HOW TO HELP THE PLANET

KEEPING ECOSYSTEMS CLEAN

by
Rebecca Phillips-Bartlett

Minneapolis, Minnesota

Credits: All images are courtesy of Shutterstock.com, unless otherwise specified. With thanks to Getty Images, Thinkstock Photo, and iStockphoto. Recurring images – VectorMine, Anna Kosheleva. Cover – VectorMine, Tatevosian Yana. 2–3 – Trofimov Denis. 4–5 – ESB Professionali, Larina Marina 6–7 – wavebreakmedia. 8–9 – tomfotorama, Tanja Esser, Oya.Oraya Tepa, aguscrespophoto. 10–11 – Monkey Business Images, Mikhail Sedov, Daniel Chetroni. 12–13 – vchal, chansont. 14–15 – Wavebreakmedia, Rawpixel.com, Yuliya Evstratenko, Switlana Sonyashna. 16–17 – Jinning Li, Sergey Ryzhov. 18–19 – lomiso, Jerome.Romme. 20–21 – Rawpixel.com, Pressmaster. 22–23 – Rawpixel.com, rangizzz.

Bearport Publishing Company Product Development Team
President: Jen Jenson; Director of Product Development: Spencer Brinker; Managing Editor: Allison Juda; Associate Editor: Naomi Reich; Associate Editor: Tiana Tran; Senior Designer: Colin O'Dea; Designer: Elena Klinkner; Designer: Kayla Eggert; Product Development Assistant: Owen Hamlin

Library of Congress Cataloging-in-Publication Data

Names: Phillips-Bartlett, Rebecca, 1999- author.
Title: Keeping ecosystems clean / by Rebecca Phillips-Bartlett.
Description: Minneapolis, Minnesota : Bearport Publishing Company, [2024] | Series: How to help the planet | Includes index.
Identifiers: LCCN 2023031015 (print) | LCCN 2023031016 (ebook) | ISBN 9798889162841 (library binding) | ISBN 9798889162896 (paperback) | ISBN 9798889162933 (ebook)
Subjects: LCSH: Sustainable living--Juvenile literature.
Classification: LCC GE195.5 .P49 2024 (print) | LCC GE195.5 (ebook) | DDC 304.2--dc23/eng/20230817
LC record available at https://lccn.loc.gov/2023031015
LC ebook record available at https://lccn.loc.gov/2023031016

© 2024 BookLife Publishing
This edition is published by arrangement with BookLife Publishing.

North American adaptations © 2024 Bearport Publishing Company. All rights reserved. No part of this publication may be reproduced in whole or in part, stored in any retrieval system, or transmitted in any form or by any means, electronic, mechanical, photocopying, recording, or otherwise, without written permission from the publisher.

For more information, write to Bearport Publishing, 5357 Penn Avenue South, Minneapolis, MN 55419.

CONTENTS

Our Planet, Our Home 4
There Is Plenty We Can Do 6
What Is an Ecosystem? 8
How to Live with Nature 10
How to Avoid Waste 12
How to Help in the Garden 14
How to Eat Green 16
How to Try Composting 18
How to Spread the Word 20
We Can Help 22
Glossary 24
Index 24

OUR PLANET, OUR HOME

Earth is our home. It gives us everything we need to live. The planet takes care of us, but we are not always good at taking care of it.

We have made the planet unhealthy with lots of **pollution**. These are things we make and leave around that make Earth dirty. What can we do to help fight pollution?

Pollution can be on the ground, in the oceans, and in the air.

THERE IS PLENTY WE CAN DO

Pollution is a problem, but there is plenty we can do to clean up the planet. Even the smallest things can make a difference.

Picking up trash off the ground is a great start!

Living things and nonliving things are all a part of **ecosystems**. We have a **responsibility** to look after the planet's ecosystems. We also have the power to protect them.

WHAT IS AN ECOSYSTEM?

Ecosystems have many living things, such as animals and plants. An ecosystem's nonliving things, such as its water and soil, are also very important.

The things in an ecosystem need one another to stay healthy. An ecosystem is healthiest when things are in **balance**.

TOO DRY

TOO WET

JUST RIGHT

An ecosystem needs just the right amount of rain for plants to grow.

9

HOW TO LIVE WITH NATURE

Getting outside is a great way to learn more about the planet. Go for a walk in nature! As we head outdoors, we can do our part to keep ecosystems clean.

Stick to the trail when you go out in nature.

Leaving trash behind is called **littering**. It is one of the ways humans harm Earth. Pick up any litter you see, and make sure to take your trash away with you.

LITTER

HOW TO AVOID WASTE

Trash is piled up in landfills and then covered in dirt.

When we throw away trash, it does not just disappear. A lot of it goes to **landfills**. These big piles of garbage are bad for Earth.

Landfills add waste to ecosystems. This can change the balance of life there. Keep things out of landfills by **recycling** or reusing them. Try selling or donating things you are done with.

HOW TO HELP IN THE GARDEN

A garden is an ecosystem, too! Whether you have a big backyard or a small pot with dirt, you can help the planet by growing flowers.

Try growing plants to help your backyard ecosystem!

Flowers make food for bees, and bees help the plants grow. Then, plants help us by cleaning the air.

HOW TO EAT GREEN

What we put on our plate can help the planet, too. Some kinds of farming can hurt ecosystems. Farmers may spray their plants with **chemicals**.

Farm chemicals can easily spread around an ecosystem.

Other farms harm ecosystems by taking too much out of them. They may use lots of water or get rid of other plants in the area. Eat local foods from farmers that take care of their land. It's good for you and Earth!

HOW TO TRY COMPOSTING

COMPOSTING

You can even help an ecosystem with the food you don't eat. **Composting** breaks down food and turns it into dirt.

Dirt from composting is great for growing new plants. Getting rid of your food scraps in this way also means sending less waste to landfills!

When composting, use only uncooked plant parts.

HOW TO SPREAD THE WORD

All the little things you do to help Earth really add up. Imagine what could happen if even more people knew how to help!

Teach your friends about taking care of Earth's ecosystems! You could make a poster with all that you have learned.

Draw pictures of litter, landfills, flowers, farming, or composting!

WE CAN HELP

Pollution is a big problem for our planet's ecosystems. However, the ways we live, eat, and get rid of used things all make a difference.

Together, we can help the planet and protect our ecosystems from pollution. Small things we do can make a big change!

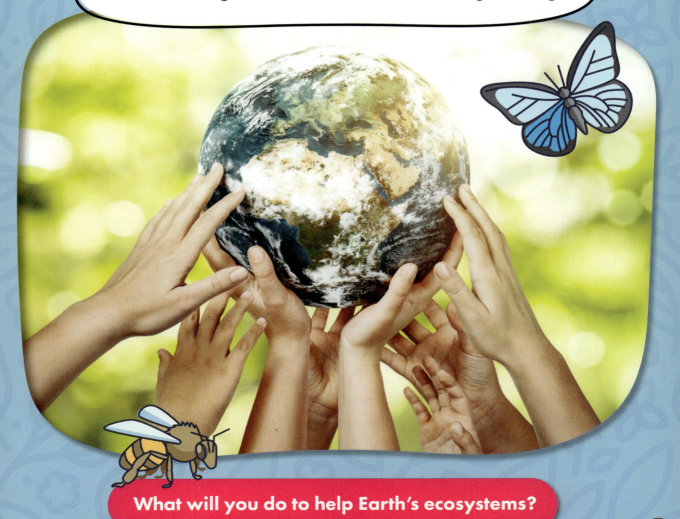

What will you do to help Earth's ecosystems?

GLOSSARY

balance having the right amount of a mix of things

chemicals natural or human-made substances that can harm living things

composting gathering food scraps so they can be turned into dirt

ecosystems groups of living and nonliving things that make up an environment and affect one another

landfills pits where waste is dumped and then covered by soil

littering leaving trash in nature

pollution anything that makes Earth unhealthy or dirty

recycling turning something old into something new

responsibility something you are expected to do

INDEX

balance 9, 13
bees 15
composting 18–19, 21
donating 13
farming 16–17, 21
flowers 14–15, 21
food 15, 17–19
landfills 12–13, 19, 21
litter 11, 21
pollution 5–6, 22–23
recycling 13
reusing 13